Where Is the Brooklyn Bridge?

by Megan Stine

illustrated by John Hinderliter

Grosset & Dunlap
An Imprint of Penguin Random House

For my father, who once designed a bridge and taught me to be excited about engineering—MS

GROSSET & DUNLAP
Penguin Young Readers Group
An Imprint of Penguin Random House LLC

Text copyright © 2016 by Megan Stine. Illustrations copyright © 2016 by Penguin Random House LLC. All rights reserved. Published by Grosset & Dunlap, an imprint of Penguin Random House LLC, 345 Hudson Street, New York, New York 10014. GROSSET & DUNLAP is a trademark of Penguin Random House LLC. Printed in the USA.

Library of Congress Cataloging-in-Publication Data is available.

ISBN 978-0-448-48424-2   10 9 8 7 6 5 4 3 2 1

Contents

Where Is the Brooklyn Bridge?

New York City

It was a bitterly cold day in the winter of 1853. The wind beat against the passengers on a ferryboat. The boat was trapped in the East River, stuck between huge chunks of ice. But the passengers had to put up with it. The ferryboat was the only practical way to get from New York City to Brooklyn. New York was an island, surrounded on all sides by water. In those days, nearly everyone who came to New York, or left it, traveled by boat.

Fifteen-year-old Washington Roebling was on the ferry that day with his father, John Roebling. At forty-six, John Roebling was the most famous bridge builder in America. He was a genius and

John Roebling

a gentleman. He was also a very tough man. He had strong opinions and not much patience. If someone was even five minutes late for an appointment, he'd cancel the meeting and send the person away! For a man like John Roebling to be stuck for hours on a boat—doing nothing, wasting time—was pure torture.

It was especially hard for Roebling since all he had to do was look around and he could imagine a better way to travel. *There should be a bridge here.*

A bridge connecting New York and Brooklyn. Right there and then, he imagined the Brooklyn Bridge in his mind's eye. But it would take thirty more years before the bridge would be finished—and John Roebling would be long dead.

CHAPTER 1
We Need a Bridge

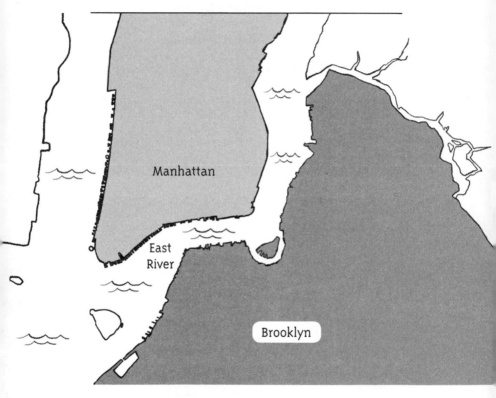

In the 1860s, Brooklyn was a separate city. It did not become part of New York City until 1898. In fact, Brooklyn had grown to be the third largest city in the country.

Everyone knew that New York City was a much more exciting place, but not everyone could afford it. Besides, New York City was very crowded, except for open pastures far uptown where no one ever expected to live. Downtown, there were low houses and other buildings covering nearly all the land. If more people wanted to live in New York, where would they go?

No one could imagine that someday New York City would be full of skyscrapers. The city would grow *up*! Toward the sky! Back in the late 1800s, everyone thought that when New York was full, people would spill into Brooklyn. There was plenty of room in Brooklyn for new houses, factories, and shops.

The only problem was those ferries. In bad weather, they were slow. Sometimes they didn't run at all!

For years and years, people had hoped for a bridge across the East River. But there were difficulties. First of all, the river was always full of boats and tall ships. The boats were extremely important. They brought food, lumber, tools, and people to the city each day. If a bridge were to be built across the river, it would have to be very tall, so the ships could sail under it.

People also worried about the cost of a bridge and how the city would pay for it. A bridge would cost millions of dollars. Back then many workers earned only one or two dollars a day.

Most of all, people worried about whether a bridge would be safe. Was it possible to build a sturdy, strong bridge that would reach all the way across the wide river? One that would be high enough over the water to allow for all the boats sailing under it?

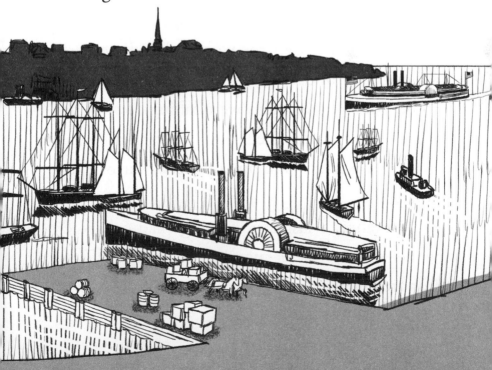

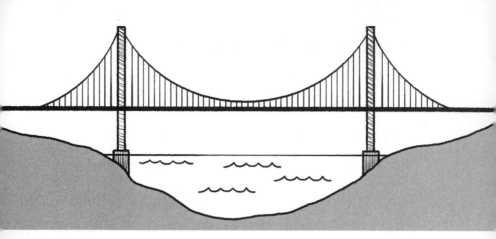

The only kind of bridge that would be high enough for all the boats was called a suspension bridge. A suspension bridge holds up a roadway with huge, thick cables. Many suspension bridges had been built all over the world—but none were as long as a bridge over the East River needed to be. And a lot of them were falling down! The engineers who designed and built them were making mistakes. One out of every four bridges collapsed!

In France, a suspension bridge had collapsed while soldiers were marching across it. Two hundred men died.

In America, a small bridge in Kentucky collapsed while a herd of cattle was crossing it. And everyone knew about the problems with a bridge in Wheeling, West Virginia. In 1854, just five years after it was built, a big wind came along. The whole bridge twisted up into the air like a ribbon in the wind!

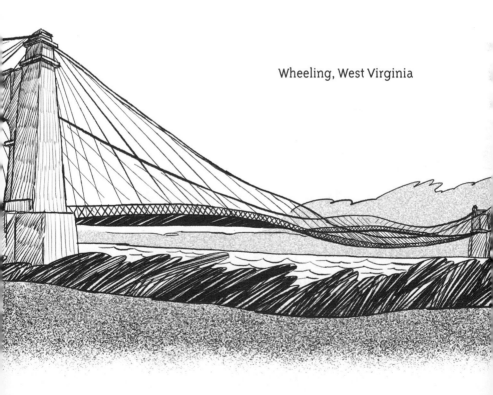

Wheeling, West Virginia

But John Roebling was sure he could build a bridge that wouldn't fall. He owned a wire company. And using wire—thick, strong ropes of it—was one of the keys to building a good suspension bridge. He had already built three wonderful bridges using wire. If he could just show people his other bridges, he felt sure they would have faith in his plan.

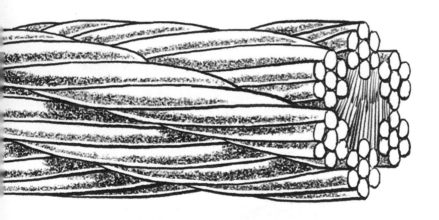

In April 1869, Roebling took a group of twenty-two people on a trip called the "Bridge Party." The group included engineers who thought the Brooklyn Bridge couldn't be built.

It also included businessmen and politicians who
very much wanted it. By train, they traveled to
Pittsburgh, Cincinnati, and Niagara Falls. They
went to see the three suspension bridges that John
Roebling had built using huge cables made out of
wire.

In Pittsburgh, Pennsylvania, Roebling showed off his most beautiful bridge. It had tall, fancy iron towers. The sides of the bridge had hundreds of crisscrossing wires that looked like the bars of a cage or netting.

In Cincinnati, Ohio, he showed them the longest suspension bridge in the world at the time. It crossed the Ohio River and was 1,057 feet long. It took no time for horse-drawn carriages to get across it. It was also a wonderful place to walk and enjoy the river. When the "Bridge Party" walked on the bridge, they could feel how sturdy it was.

But the best stop of the trip was the visit to Niagara Falls in New York State. There, John Roebling's bridge was suspended high above the Niagara River, with the famous waterfalls in the background. The scenery was incredible. Better yet, the bridge had an important extra feature: It was strong enough for a train to go across!

When the trip was over, all the experts agreed that John Roebling was the right man to build the Brooklyn Bridge.

It wasn't called the Brooklyn Bridge at first, though. One idea was to name it the Empire Bridge. Or the East River Bridge. For a while, everyone just called it the Great Bridge.

John Roebling went to work right away. He had already designed the bridge. It was going to have two tall stone towers. The towers would hold up thick cables, and the cables would hold up the roadway. Now he hired engineers to draw designs of the bridge's different parts. He hired more engineers to oversee the carpenters, masons, and builders who would do the actual work. Hundreds of men would be needed over the months and years to build the bridge.

Roebling also needed someone in charge of all the workers to make sure the bridge was built correctly. His son, Washington Roebling, had graduated from the best engineering college in America, called Rensselaer Polytechnic Institute. So Roebling decided his son would be his right-

Washington Roebling

hand man. Perhaps one day his son would take over and be in charge of building the bridge.

Washington Roebling moved to a house in Brooklyn Heights, near the river. That way, he would live just a few blocks from the work site. John Roebling spent most days at his home in Trenton, New Jersey. It was right beside his wire factory.

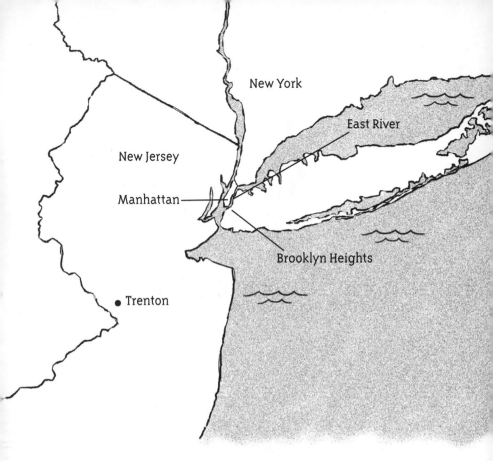

When the final plans for the bridge were approved on June 25, 1869, John Roebling came to Brooklyn.

Three days later, he and his son went down to the East River to discuss locations for the bridge. John was standing at the end of the ferry slip—

right at the edge of the river where the ferryboat docked. As the huge ferry hit the wooden pilings, it smashed into his foot. John Roebling collapsed to the ground. His foot was crushed!

His son quickly took him to a doctor nearby. It was a terrible injury. His toes had to be cut off!

Roebling let the doctors do it right away. Then he insisted on wrapping up his foot himself.

He was so stubborn, he wouldn't do what the doctors told him to do. He fired two doctors and bossed around the third one. He thought he knew better than everyone else.

For a few days, it seemed like John Roebling might be okay. He stayed at his son's house in Brooklyn Heights. But then, instead of getting better, he started getting worse. He had horrible headaches. He couldn't eat. He couldn't even open his mouth! His face was frozen. Every so often, his body would suddenly twist into painful shapes.

The doctors knew what was wrong. Roebling had a disease called lockjaw. It is also known as tetanus. There was no cure for it in those days, because this was long before medicines such as penicillin had been discovered.

A few weeks later, on July 22, 1869, John Roebling died. He was gone before work on his most important bridge had even begun.

CHAPTER 2
Like Father, Like Son

A huge funeral was held at John Roebling's home in Trenton, New Jersey. The whole town showed up. Two thousand people stood on the lawn in front of his house to honor him.

Fifty or so important men came from Brooklyn and New York City, too—politicians, builders, and engineers. The train pulled up right in front of the Roebling house!

When the funeral was over, the men from Brooklyn all agreed that thirty-two-year-old Washington Roebling should take over building the bridge. He had helped his father build the Cincinnati Bridge. He had also helped his father draw up the plans for the Brooklyn Bridge.

Washington Roebling was like his father in many ways. He was smart, honest, and very sure of himself. But while his father was strict and stern, Washington was kind and gentle. His father had a bad temper. Washington was easygoing and calm.

After college, Washington Roebling had gone to work in his father's wire factory. In fact, he ran it for a while when he was only twenty years old!

Then the Civil War broke out, in 1861. Washington joined the Union Army in the fight against the Southern states that had broken away from the country. At the age of twenty-four, Washington was an officer in charge of building bridges.

One time, his job was to build a bridge across the Shenandoah River in Virginia. But how wide was the river? There were no boats to sail across the river with a measuring tape. So Washington attached one end of the tape to the shore. Then he swam across the river himself—with the tape in his mouth!

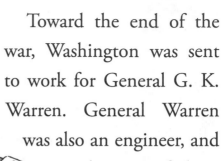

Toward the end of the war, Washington was sent to work for General G. K. Warren. General Warren was also an engineer, and the two of them built bridges for use during the war.

At a party for officers, Washington fell in love with the general's sister, Emily Warren. She liked him, too. He was handsome and kind, with blue-gray eyes, light hair, and a sharp mind.

Emily was perfect for Washington. She was graceful and intelligent.

Best of all, she loved science. She understood all the details about bridge building when Washington explained them to her.

Six weeks after the ball, they were engaged. And on January 18, 1865, Washington and Emily were married. They had a double wedding ceremony with another one of her brothers and his bride.

In 1867, Emily became pregnant with their first and only child. That same year, John Roebling sent Washington and Emily to Europe to look at bridges there. John Roebling paid for the whole trip! He knew he was going to build the Brooklyn Bridge soon—or at least he hoped so! He wanted his son to learn all about caissons. Caissons were the heavy foundations, or bases, that went under bridge towers. They were a new idea. A few bridge

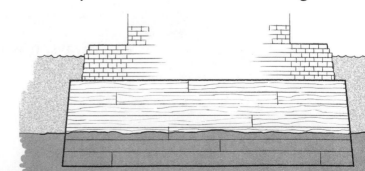

Caisson

builders in Europe had been using them for about twenty years.

While Washington and Emily were in Europe, their son was born on November 21, 1867. They named him John A. Roebling II.

For several months, Washington and Emily traveled all over Europe. They talked to bridge engineers everywhere they went. When they came back to America, Washington knew more about caissons than his father did!

It was a good thing, too. Because when it was time to start building the bridge, John Roebling was already dead. Washington Roebling took over the job. He would be the chief engineer.

He had no idea it would be the most dangerous job he would ever do—or that, in some ways, it would ruin his life.

CHAPTER 3
How to Build a Suspension Bridge

Washington knew how to build a suspension bridge. He knew how to build towers, cables, and a roadway. In some ways, that was the easy part. The hard part was the very first step—building the caissons. Those were the bases that went deep into the river, under the towers. That had to be done before anything else.

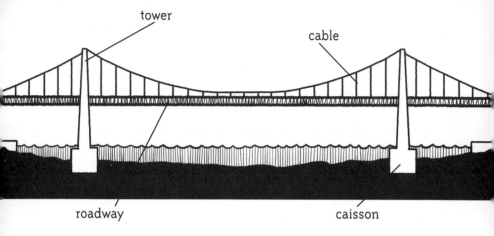

tower

cable

roadway

caisson

A suspension bridge is different from other kinds of bridges. On a suspension bridge, the weight of the roadway is suspended—or held up—by wires attached to cables.

There are three main parts that you can see when you look at a suspension bridge—the towers, the cables, and the roadway. You can also see thin wire ropes. But you can't see the caissons, because they're underwater.

The first step is to put the caissons in place, and then build two tall towers on top of them—one on each side of the river. The towers have to be very tall, so that the roadway will be high above the river to allow boats to pass under it. The towers also have to be very solid and strong. Why? Because all the weight of the bridge will be pressing down on them.

The second step is to make the huge cables that hold up the roadway. The cables have to be strong enough to hold up the weight of the bridge and not break. The cables are made up of thousands of pieces of thin wire. Each wire is less than a quarter of an inch thick. But when thousands of wires are wrapped together, they become one huge, thick cable. In the Brooklyn Bridge, the cables are almost sixteen inches thick! Most suspension bridges have either two or four huge main cables. The Brooklyn Bridge has four.

Dangling straight down from the cables are lots of pieces of wire rope. Those ropes are called the suspenders. Like a pair of suspenders that hold up pants, they hold up the floor of the bridge. They are wrapped around the cables, and they attach to the roadway—just like the ropes of a swing are attached to the seat. The roadway actually hangs down from all those ropes or suspenders like the seat of a swing.

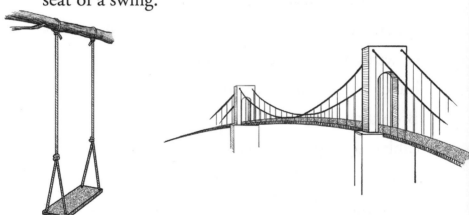

The third step in building a bridge is to make the roadway. A roadway is made up of a lot of sections of steel. Each piece is hung from the ropes and cables, one piece at a time.

But wait—what keeps the cables from falling down? What are they attached to? The huge cables rest on the towers, but they aren't really attached to the towers. The cables are attached—or anchored—to a large building on the land. The building is called an anchorage. There are two anchorages, one on each side of the river.

When the cables are made, the wires are wrapped around some metal bars that are buried inside the anchorage. The metal bars are held in place by tons and tons of stone. With enough stone on top, the bars can't move. The wires can't move. So the cables of the bridge can't go anywhere!

Building the towers would have to be Washington's first step. But before he could build the towers, he had to build the bases for the towers—the caissons. That was the most dangerous step. It was where so many things could go wrong. And so many things did.

Other Suspension Bridges

The Brooklyn Bridge was the longest suspension bridge in the world when it was built. The distance between the two towers was 1,595 feet. That's about six blocks long. Twenty years later, a longer

bridge opened on the East River. It was called the Williamsburg Bridge. Then the Manhattan Bridge was built. By 1909, there were three bridges connecting Brooklyn and the island of Manhattan.

The longest suspension bridge in the United States today is called the Verrazano-Narrows Bridge. It connects two parts of New York City—Brooklyn and Staten Island. It is 4,260 feet long. The second longest in the United States is the Golden Gate Bridge in San Francisco, which is 4,200 feet long.

Where is the longest suspension bridge in the world? Japan! It's the Akashi-Kaiky Bridge, also called the Pearl Bridge. The whole bridge is more than two miles long!

Golden Gate Bridge

CHAPTER 4
The Deadly Caissons

In March 1870, the first caisson was ready to be launched into the East River like a boat.

The caisson was like a building—without a floor! It was 168 feet long and 102 feet wide—as big as two basketball courts! The roof of the caisson was five feet thick at first. After it was launched, more wood was added to the roof to make it even thicker. When it was finished, the roof was fifteen feet thick. The whole thing weighed six million pounds!

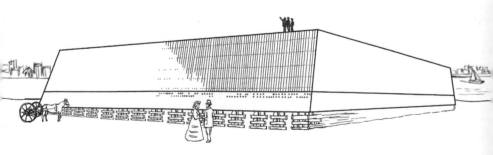

It had been built by a shipbuilder because, in some ways, a caisson was a lot like an upside-down ship. It had to be waterproof, like a ship. And it had to float like a ship—at least at first. It had to be sturdy enough to hold the weight of a huge stone bridge tower. But it also had to have a room inside, so men could work underwater.

Once the caisson was floating on the river, it would be moved into place. Washington Roebling would say exactly where the caisson should go.

Then huge pieces of stone would be piled up on top of it, to make it heavy. Pretty soon, it would sink to the bottom of the river.

The "room" inside the caisson would fill up with water at first, since there was no floor in the caisson. The river bottom was the "floor." But Washington Roebling had a plan. He had big machines that would force air—called compressed air—into the space. The air would push all the water out! Then men could climb down into the room from above and be able to breathe inside.

How Compressed Air Moves Water—Try It!

Here's a trick you can do to show how compressed air moved water out of a caisson.

Fill a mug with water almost to the top. Set the mug on a kitchen counter. Blow up a balloon, but don't tie a knot in it. Hold the balloon's neck closed with your fingers. Slide the neck into the water, and hold it under. Now let the air out and watch what happens!

The air pushed some of the water up and out of the mug, didn't it? That's how the compressed air pushed water out of the huge caisson. Of course it took a lot more than a balloon to force water out of a caisson. It took six big machines with huge motors. But with all the air compressors running, all the water in the caisson was emptied out in just a few hours.

Once men were inside the caisson, they could dig out the floor of the river. Little by little, as they dug, the caisson would settle into riverbed, lower and lower. Finally it would reach solid rock—called bedrock. Then the caisson would be filled with concrete. The base for the towers would be solid and safe.

The company that built the first caisson thought the whole idea was a little crazy. They weren't even sure it would work. So they insisted on being paid in advance.

No one even knew if the first caisson would

float after it was launched into the river. But it did! About three thousand people came to watch.

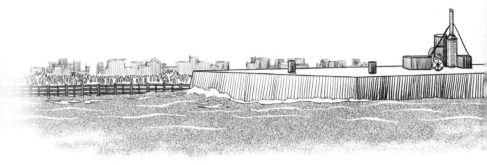

Washington Roebling was there every single day to make sure things went well.

But almost from the start, it was a scary, dangerous job.

On the first day, a crew of men climbed down into a tube. It was like an elevator shaft that led down into the caisson. In the tube, there was a small space with doors at the top and bottom. It was an airlock. The airlock kept compressed air inside the caisson. Compressed air wasn't like regular air, though. It pressed on people's bodies harder than the air outside.

When a dozen men were inside the airlock, they closed the top door tight. Then they opened a little hole from below. It let the compressed air into the airlock chamber. All of a sudden, there was a terrible screeching noise, like a steam whistle.

The pressure hurt their ears, like the pressure on an airplane can hurt sometimes. Only worse. It hurt their heads, too. It felt like they might explode! The men wanted to leave

immediately. But they didn't. They were being paid good money—two dollars a day!

So the men stood it for as long as they could. They went into the caisson and got to work.

The air pressure had a strange effect on them, though. For one thing, it changed their voices. Inside the caisson, their voices sounded high-pitched, like girls' voices. They couldn't whistle in the caisson, either. It also made them extremely hungry—hungrier than they'd ever been.

It was hot down there, too, and very humid. People started sweating right away, even if they weren't doing any work.

Newspapers wrote about the workers in the caisson. They said they were either heroes or fools. It seemed so dangerous to go work underneath the water! And what were they doing down there? From the banks of the river, no one could see a thing.

Every day, more than two hundred men went down into the caissons. Their main job was to dig into the river bottom, so the caisson would settle into it. They had to dig out huge boulders and break them into small pieces with sledgehammers. Then the boulders were sent up to the top through tubes.

Other things were sent up through tubes, too. Since there was no bathroom in the caisson, the men used a wooden box filled halfway with water as a toilet. To empty the toilet, they put a tube in it that ran up through the roof. The air pressure in the tube would suck all the poop up to the surface—and spray it into the air!

As the men dug out the river, the caisson sank. As the caisson sank, workers aboveground added stone blocks to the top of it, for the towers. That way, there was always some stone sticking up, above the waterline. Little by the little, the caisson was sinking and the tower was being built. But most of the tower was still underwater.

The work underground was filthy and hard. The men were standing in river muck. They had candles for lights, as well as limelights—a kind of special gaslight used at that time on theater stages—but any kind of flame was dangerous. The compressed air made it more likely that things would explode.

It took months to dig out the river floor. And some of the men who worked in the caisson were starting to get sick.

No one in America at the time knew the real reason why.

CHAPTER 5
The Bends

The longer the men worked in the caissons, the sicker some of them got. They would come up out of the caisson and collapse on the ground in pain. Sometimes they vomited. Sometimes, their legs or arms hurt terribly. Sometimes they couldn't see properly. Some men couldn't even walk. They could be paralyzed for a few days!

But they never felt any pain when they were down in the caisson—only after they came back up to dry land.

The men didn't get sick until after a few weeks on the job. So it seemed the sickness was from spending too much time down there.

But that was only part of the problem.

The men were suffering from what we now call "the bends." Deep-sea divers get the bends if they come up to the surface too fast. And the deeper the dive, the more slowly they need to come back up.

The same was true for the men in the caissons. At first, the caisson wasn't very deep—so the air pressure wasn't very strong. But as the caisson sank, it took more compressed air to push the water out of the big room. The deeper the caisson went, the more slowly the men should have come up to the surface. They should have stayed in the airlock for at least twenty minutes, so their bodies could adjust to the change in air pressure.

But they didn't.

Pretty soon, men started quitting the job. Washington Roebling couldn't blame them. He could see they were in bad shape.

Then one night in December 1870, something awful happened. Men were in the caisson on the night shift. One of the workers held a candle too near the ceiling. The seams between the ceiling planks were sealed with oakum, which is twisted rope coated with black tar that burned easily.

Suddenly, the caisson was on fire!

The men tried to put out the fire. They threw buckets of water up into the air. They used fire extinguishers. They stuffed wet rags into the hole where the fire was burning. Finally they brought hoses down into the caisson, to pump water at the fire.

At first that seemed to work. But the compressed air inside the caisson made the fire burn superfast. It burned deep into the thick wooden ceiling of the caisson—like a river of fire running through the wood.

Washington Roebling came running as soon as he heard the news. He had been down in the caisson all day, but had gone home. Now he was going to be down there all night. He wanted to make sure the fire was really out. He had men drill holes into the ceiling. Even though no one could see the fire, Washington knew it was probably still burning somewhere inside the roof.

For hours, Washington worked calmly to help put out the fire. When the fire finally seemed to be out, he went back to the surface.

But the minute he came up, he collapsed. He couldn't feel his legs. He couldn't walk! He was completely exhausted and weak. It was his first time getting the bends—but it wouldn't be his last.

When the Brooklyn caisson reached forty-five feet deep, it hit solid rock. Now it was safe to continue building the tall stone tower on top of it. When each tower was done, it would stand 276½ feet above the water. Of course there was already a lot of stone below the water, resting on the caisson, which no one could see.

Two months later, a second caisson was launched. This one was for the tower on the New York side of the river. Washington and his wife, Emily, rode on it like a boat! They felt perfectly safe standing on it, waving to people who watched from shore.

Soon, men were working in the New York caisson, digging away. The digging went more quickly this time. The riverbed wasn't so rocky on the New York side—it was just sand. It was easy to dig out the sand and shoot it up through the tubes to the surface. Ten to fourteen men in the caisson would stand around a tube, shoveling sand toward it as fast as they could. The tube sucked the sand up into the air.

But as soon as the caisson reached forty-five feet deep, the workers started to get sick with the bends. And this time, the job was only half done. The New York caisson would need to go twice as deep as the Brooklyn caisson to reach solid rock. It would have to be about ninety feet deep!

A few weeks later, Washington Roebling hired a doctor to try to figure out why the men were getting so sick. One man fell to the ground, bleeding from his ears and nose! More than a hundred men got the bends. Many of them quit the job.

When the caisson reached seventy-one feet deep, two men died from the bends. One of the men had only been on the job for one day. He had worked in the caisson only a few hours when he got sick. He went home and dropped dead outside his bedroom.

A few days later, a third man started vomiting and was still vomiting a day later. Everyone, including Washington, was terribly upset. The workers went out on strike. They demanded higher pay and got it. The work continued a few weeks longer, but more men were getting the bends.

When a third man died, Washington Roebling made a decision. He stopped the digging. He couldn't ask the men to dig any deeper. He didn't want more men to die.

But the caisson was still sitting on gravel and sand. Was the caisson's resting place solid enough to hold up the tower?

Washington certainly hoped so.

CHAPTER 6
A Man in His Room

By the time the caissons were finished, Washington Roebling was a wreck. This first stage of the project had taken more than two years. He had worked twelve hours or more six days a week. He had gone down to the caissons and come back up hundreds of times. He knew every detail about the bridge and was in charge of it all. But all the work and the number of tragedies were ruining his health.

In the spring of 1872, Washington got the bends again and collapsed. This time, the pain was so terrible he had to stay in bed for days.

The doctors thought he would die.

In the following months, his health got worse. Finally, Washington was too sick to leave his house. He could barely speak or eat. Emily sometimes had to feed him. He had terrible headaches. Some days, he couldn't see well. Was he going blind? He couldn't write, either. His handwriting was a messy scrawl. He felt too nervous to meet with his assistants. He didn't want to talk to anyone.

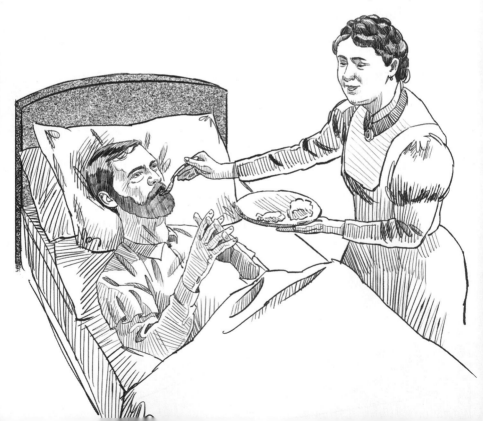

The truth was, Washington Roebling was having a nervous breakdown. The stress of building the bridge was ruining his health.

Little by little, Emily began to take over speaking and writing for her husband. Whenever the bridge workers needed to know what to do next, they would ask Emily. She would talk to Washington and then give them an answer. She wrote all her husband's letters for him, putting down exactly what he wanted to say.

Meanwhile, Washington sat near a window in his house in Brooklyn. His house faced the river.

With a pair of binoculars, he was able to watch construction of the bridge. He also had a telescope mounted by the window. He saw everything that went on. His mind was sharp, even though his spirit and body were broken. He just didn't want to see other people or talk to them—maybe not ever again.

As for the towers, it took five years to build them. It was slow work, and sometimes dangerous, but it wasn't very hard. So for six months, Washington and Emily went on a trip to Europe. Perhaps a vacation would make him feel better. It didn't. Finally they moved back into his father's house in Trenton, New Jersey. From there, Washington wrote letters to the men who were working on the bridge. He was still the chief engineer.

Washington and Emily stayed in New Jersey for nearly three years, until the two bridge towers were built. Then they moved to New York, then back to Brooklyn. He still didn't want to go out of the house or see people, but he wanted to be nearby. He still loved his job.

Over time, all the men on the bridge job came to respect Emily Roebling. They treated her as an equal. That was very unusual then. The workers at the bridge didn't mind when Emily

came to check and make sure a job was being done correctly. Once, a bridge engineer came to Washington's house with a problem. Instead of discussing it with her husband, Emily sat down with the engineer herself. She did a small drawing to show him how to solve the problem.

People began to think Emily was the real brains behind the bridge. She certainly was brilliant—but her husband was still very much in charge. He kept every single detail about the bridge in his head. He still made all the plans and drawings.

Finally it was time to start putting the wire cables in place. That was going to be a very tricky, very important part of the job. Washington was looking forward to it. He knew more about wire than almost anyone else. He and his father had always thought their company would make the wire for the bridge.

Unfortunately, other men had different ideas about who should make the wire—and who should make a lot of money from it, too.

CHAPTER 7
Greed

There was a lot of money to be made building the Brooklyn Bridge.

Many businessmen hoped to get rich supplying the materials for the bridge. They wanted to sell stone for the towers, steel for the roadway, and the wire for the cables.

Even before the work started, there were politicians who wanted to get rich from the bridge, too. In New York at that time, many politicians were dishonest. They took bribes before okaying many city projects. If the Brooklyn Bridge was going to be built, the politicians wanted to be kept happy.

Boss Tweed

The most famous dishonest politician in New York City was a man named William M. Tweed who was the "boss" of the Democratic Party. He controlled nearly all the Democrats who were elected to office. Everyone called him Boss Tweed. Whenever banks or businesses wanted a certain law passed that would help them make money, they had to bribe Boss Tweed. Whenever someone wanted to build a public building, they had to double the price—and then give Boss Tweed half of the profits!

Boss Tweed was so rich, he owned land and buildings all over New York City. He owned a huge hotel. He was a big shot at several companies— a bank, a railroad, and a printing company. Even the mayor and the governor of New York took orders from him! Everyone knew they had better go along with Boss Tweed, or nothing would get done.

It was no different with the Brooklyn Bridge. To get permission to build the bridge, a law had to be passed. So Boss Tweed had to be paid. He got more than fifty thousand dollars in cash. It was taken to him from Brooklyn in a carpetbag!

While in power, Boss Tweed stole more than $75 million from New York. Finally, however, he was brought to justice and died in jail. Before his death, he confessed to all his crimes. He admitted that the Brooklyn Bridge was one of his crooked deals.

Besides politicians, some men in charge of building the bridge were willing to cheat to make more money. They gave out jobs to friends who would help them make money.

When it was time to decide who should make the wire for the bridge cables, a man named J. Lloyd Haigh got the job. He planned to charge way too much for the cheap, faulty wire he was going to make. That way he'd make a lot of money. Then he'd hand over some of the extra cash to the man who gave him the job. Giving money back this way is called a "kickback."

This upset Washington Roebling for two reasons. For one thing, he really wanted the job. It only seemed right that his father's wire company make the wire for a bridge he and his father had designed.

But he also wanted the bridge to be built safely and correctly. And he knew that Haigh was not an honest man. Washington was afraid that

Haigh would make bad wire. So he told the men in charge to make sure to test every single batch of wire that came from Haigh.

Even so, Haigh managed to get around the wire tests. He used several tricks. For example, he would let a wire inspector test a good batch of wire. As soon as it passed the test, he put it on a cart and pretended to drive it to the bridge. But as soon as the cart was out of sight, Haigh took the good wire off the cart—and put bad wire on! He sent the good wire back to his own factory. He sent the bad wire directly to the bridge!

The next day, Haigh would do the same thing all over again. He showed one batch of good wire to the inspector—and then sent bad wire to the bridge.

Fortunately, Washington found out, and he was furious. However, bad wire was already being woven into the bridge cables! Every day, thin strands of wire were being pulled back and forth, across the towers, to make the huge cables. There was no way to get it out.

Washington wanted Haigh fired. But the men in charge wouldn't do it. They didn't want to admit their mistake in giving Haigh the job.

The bad wire was so poorly made, it snapped in half—like breaking a piece of uncooked spaghetti! What if the bridge cables snapped in half? The whole roadway would fall down!

But Washington realized that the bridge

would be okay, as long as they used good wire from now on. The bridge had been designed to be six times stronger than it needed to be! Now it would only be five times stronger. That was still good enough.

After Haigh was caught cheating, the wire inspectors watched him like a hawk. They made sure every batch of wire was good. Still, Haigh made an extra $300,000 from his lies and tricks. Meanwhile, Washington Roebling was only being paid $10,000 a year—and he was in charge of the whole bridge!

When the cables were finally complete in October 1878, Haigh was out of a job. A few years later, he went to prison for writing bad checks.

Now what? The next step was to wrap the huge cables in wire. After that, the workers would attach the wire suspenders that would hold up the roadway.

Who would provide the wire this time? For that job, there was only one choice—Washington Roebling. Finally, Washington was given the work, the respect, and the money he was due.

CHAPTER 8
Celebration Day

Finally, in the spring of 1883, the bridge was complete. It had cost more than $15 million to build—more than twice as much as originally planned. And it had taken fourteen years from start to finish.

There were fourteen thousand miles of wire in the cables. There were thousands of tons of stone in the towers. With all the steel in the roadway, the bridge alone weighed more than fourteen thousand tons.

The steel roadway was now in place for horses and carriages. A wooden walkway was built right down the middle of the bridge, so that people could walk across. The walkway was higher than the road. That way, people could walk above the traffic—not beside it. There were also trains built into the bridge for people who wanted to ride across. The ramps leading up to the bridge from New York and Brooklyn were also complete.

But Washington Roebling had still never set foot on the bridge. Would he go in person now?

No. He still didn't want to leave the house. He asked that Emily go in his place.

So on a spring day, before the bridge was open to the public, Emily got in a carriage in Brooklyn and rode across the bridge. She was the first person to cross the finished Brooklyn Bridge.

Then on May 24, 1883, the bridge was opened to the public. New York and Brooklyn held a huge celebration.

Thousands of people came to see the opening
of the bridge. Hotels were packed full. Restaurants
were jammed. Stores, banks, and schools were
closed for the day. Almost no one went to work!
The day was declared a holiday for all to enjoy.

Boats with flags filled the harbor. They all
tooted their whistles. Houses and store windows

were decorated for the event with flags and ribbons. Bands played everywhere.

The bridge seemed like a miracle. It stood massive and tall against the small buildings in New York and Brooklyn. It was larger than any other man-made structure at the time, except for the Great Pyramids in Egypt.

The president of the United States, Chester A. Arthur, came for the bridge opening. Governor Grover Cleveland of New York was there, too. No one knew it then, but Grover Cleveland would become the next president of the United States.

Governor Grover Cleveland

President Chester A. Arthur

At two o'clock that sunny afternoon, the president and the governor walked across the bridge from the New York side. They were accompanied by soldiers and a marching band. The mayor of Brooklyn and some important bridge officials walked from the Brooklyn side. Emily and many family members joined them. They all met in the middle and shook hands. The band played "Hail to the Chief"—a song that's always played when the president enters a room. They played it four times!

Cannons were shot off. Every boat in the harbor blasted its whistles or horns.

The bridge wasn't open to everyone yet. Seven thousand tickets had been given out to people so they could walk on the bridge that first day. Even with the tickets, people shoved and pushed. Some people's clothes got torn! Everyone wanted to see the president.

After the first day, the price was one penny to
walk across the bridge, five cents to ride a horse

across, five cents to ride the bridge train, and ten
cents to take a horse and carriage.

Washington Roebling sat at home by his window, watching the whole thing.

Would he ever get the honor and glory he deserved?

He could not bring himself to leave the house—even to meet the president. So Emily arranged for the president to come to him!

Late that afternoon, a huge party was held at their house in Brooklyn. Roses, lilacs, and calla lilies were everywhere. The stair railing was covered with flowers. The outside of the house was draped in flowers, flags, and banners, too.

A sculptor had made a bust of Washington Roebling. (A bust is a statue of someone's head.) Emily put a wreath with tiny American flags on its head.

Outside in the garden, there were tables with food and drinks. A band played music in the house, from the balcony.

When the president arrived at five thirty that afternoon, Emily and Washington greeted him. They shook hands. Washington stood and talked with the president for a few minutes. Then Washington sat on the sofa quietly, while more than a thousand people filled his house!

The president stayed for about an hour. Once he was gone, Washington was free to go back upstairs. He needed a rest. As Washington left the party, everyone burst into applause.

It was just what Emily had hoped—that the world would finally show her husband the honor and respect he deserved.

The celebration wasn't over yet, though. That night, there was an enormous fireworks display. Bands played for an hour while fourteen tons of fireworks were shot off from the bridge. Hundreds of thousands of people watched from rooftops, boats, piers, and streets. The fireworks could be seen from eighteen miles away. At the end of the fireworks, there were five hundred rockets shot off at once.

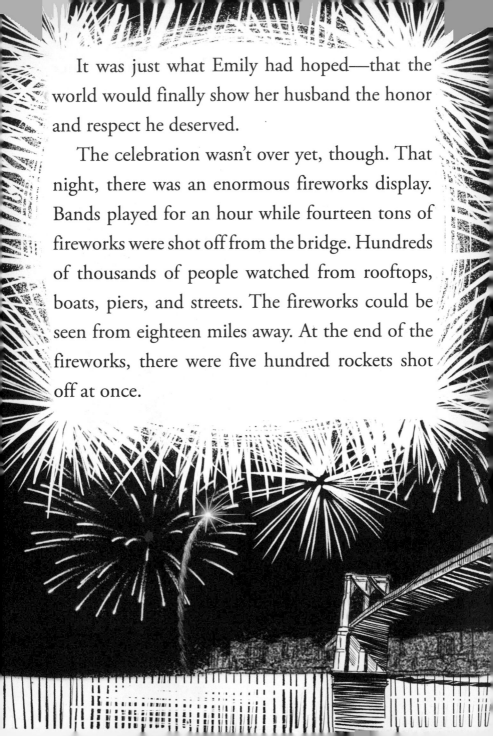

At midnight, the bridge was officially opened to everyone for a penny. Crowds of people pushed and shoved. Everyone wanted to be first. One man walked across playing the bagpipes! The city of New York didn't sleep at all that night. By morning, people were still walking across the Brooklyn Bridge. From that day on, the Brooklyn Bridge became one of the city's best-loved landmarks.

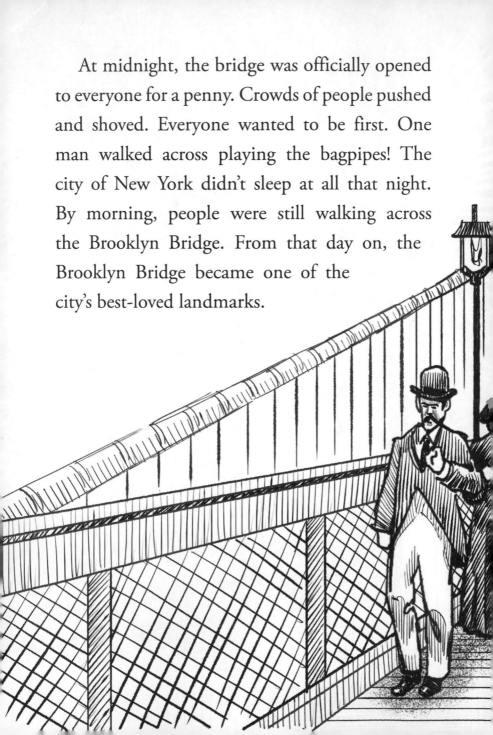

After the Bridge

Washington and Emily lived happily for many years after the bridge was built. Washington's health improved, and the two of them traveled to Europe. Their son graduated from Rensselaer—the same college Washington had attended. Emily went to college, too. She got a law degree at New York University. She also traveled to Russia alone. While she was there, the Russian tsar Nicholas was crowned and Emily was invited. Back in New York, she and Washington walked across the Brooklyn Bridge.

Emily died in 1903, but Washington lived much longer. He was a millionaire by now from the wire business and his stock investments. He was still in pain much of the time, but he married again. His second wife's name was Cornelia Farrow. In the last years of his life, he went back to running the wire company and made it even more successful. He died on July 21, 1926, at the age of eighty-nine.

CHAPTER 9
A Hundred Years of Celebrations

The Brooklyn Bridge is still famous today, more than a hundred years after it was built. Songs have been written about it. Famous artists have painted pictures of it. Movies have been shot on the bridge. And of course people have tried to get famous by doing crazy things—like jumping off the bridge!

One year after the bridge opened, P. T. Barnum took twenty-one circus elephants onto the bridge. He did it to show that the bridge was strong enough to hold a lot of weight!

A year after that, a man claimed he could jump from the bridge and survive. He jumped off wearing a red swimming suit and holding one arm straight up in the air. But he was wrong—he died from the fall.

In 1886, a man named Steve Brodie pretended to jump from the bridge, but didn't really do it. He became famous, even though a lot of people knew he was a fake. A play was written about his supposed jump, and Brodie starred in it on Broadway!

Steve Brodie

In 1919, after World War I was over, a fighter pilot flew a bomber plane under the bridge, as a prank!

When the Brooklyn Bridge was a hundred years old, New York held a huge party to celebrate.

On May 24, 1983, the most amazing fireworks display was set off from the bridge. It looked like fountains of fireworks were spraying from the towers! President Ronald Reagan was there and a parade was held. Boats filled the harbor again. New Yorkers loved it.

Today, the bridge is a favorite place for people who are in love. They bring small padlocks with their names or initials written on them. Then they lock them onto the bridge and throw the keys into the river. It's supposed to prove that their love will last forever. More than five thousand love locks were placed on the bridge in 2013 alone! Most of them are taken off, though. The bridge workers think the locks are bad for the bridge and a hazard to drivers below.

In 1964, the Brooklyn Bridge was named as a National Historic Landmark by the National Park Service. That means it has importance for the whole country. For example, the White House is also a National Historic Landmark.

THE BUILDERS OF THE BRIDGE
DEDICATED TO THE MEMORY OF
EMILY WARREN ROEBLING
1843 – 1903
WHOSE FAITH AND COURAGE HELPED HER STRICKEN HUSBAND
COL. WASHINGTON A. ROEBLING, C.E.
1837 – 1926
COMPLETE THE CONSTRUCTION OF THIS BRIDGE
FROM THE PLANS OF HIS FATHER
JOHN A. ROEBLING, C.E.
1806 – 1869
WHO GAVE HIS LIFE TO THE BRIDGE

BACK OF EVERY GREAT WORK WE CAN FIND
THE SELF-SACRIFICING DEVOTION OF A WOMAN

THIS TABLET ERECTED 1951 BY
THE BROOKLYN ENGINEERS CLUB
WITH FUNDS RAISED BY POPULAR SUBSCRIPTION

One of the best—but quietest—celebrations was the one held in 1951. That's when a plaque was added to the bridge in honor of Emily Roebling. The sign praised her "faith and courage" in helping her sick husband. It was put on the bridge by a group of engineers who knew how important she had been. It was their way of saying that without the Roeblings—John, Washington, and Emily—the Brooklyn Bridge wouldn't be what it is today.

Timeline of the Brooklyn Bridge

1806 —	John A. Roebling born in Germany on June 12
1837 —	Washington Roebling born in Pennsylvania on May 26
1851 —	John begins work on a suspension bridge in Niagara Falls
1853 —	John gets the idea for a bridge between New York and Brooklyn
1854 —	Suspension bridge collapses in Wheeling, Virginia
1861 —	Washington joins the Union Army during the Civil War and helps construct bridges
1865 —	Washington Roebling marries Emily Warren
1867 —	John A. Roebling II born to Washington and Emily on November 21
1869 —	On June 28, John is injured scouting for the bridge, becomes sick, and dies about a month later
1870 —	First caisson for the Brooklyn Bridge is launched in March; in December it catches fire
1875 —	Construction on the towers is completed
1883 —	Construction is completed on the Brooklyn Bridge; bridge opens to the public on May 24
1903 —	Emily Roebling dies
1926 —	Washington Roebling dies on July 21
1933 —	Construction begins on the Golden Gate Bridge
1964 —	Brooklyn Bridge is named a National Historic Landmark

Timeline of the World

Construction is completed on the White House	1800
Population of New York County (modern-day Manhattan) is recorded at 60,515	
The first public railways to use steam locomotives begin transporting passengers in England	1825
World's first photograph is taken	1826
Queen Victoria takes the throne	1837
John D. Rockefeller is born	1839
Edgar Allan Poe publishes *The Raven and Other Poems*	1845
Population of New York County is recorded at 515,547	1850
The *New York Times* begins publication as *New-York Daily Times*	1851
Central Park is opened	1858
Abraham Lincoln delivers Gettysburg Address on November 19	1863
First Kentucky Derby is held	1875
Alexander Graham Bell invents the telephone	1876
Population of New York County is recorded at 1,206,299	1880
President James A. Garfield assassinated	1881
Ellis Island is opened for immigrant inspection	1892
New Zealand grants women the vote, becoming the first country to do so	1893
New York, the Bronx, Brooklyn, Queens, and Staten Island consolidate to form City of Greater New York	1898
Population of New York City is recorded at 3,437,202	1900

Bibliography

*Books for young readers

"Art in the Anchorage." *Creative Time* **(blog)**,
     creativetime.org/projects/art-in-the-anchorage-1/.

"Typical Wages in 1860 Through 1890." *Outrun Change* **(blog)**,
     posted June 14, 2012, outrunchange.com/2012/06/14/typical-
     wages-in-1860-through-1890/.

Greenspan, Jesse. "Ten Things You May Not Know About the
     Brooklyn Bridge." *History.com*, posted May 23, 2013,
     history.com/news/10-things-you-may-not-know-about-the-
     brooklyn-bridge.

* Mann, Elizabeth. *The Brooklyn Bridge*. New York: Mikaya Press,
     1996.

McCullough, David. *The Great Bridge.* New York: Simon &
     Schuster, 1972.

Musumeci, Natalie. "City Wants Love-Struck Visitors to Stop
     Attaching Locks to Brooklyn Bridge." *Daily News*, posted
     May 27, 2014, nydailynews.com/new-york/brooklyn/city-
     love-struck-visitors-stop-attaching-locks-brooklyn-bridge-
     article-1.1807559.

Young, Michelle. "The Top Ten Secrets of the Brooklyn Bridge."
     Untapped Cities, posted Dec. 12, 2014, untappedcities.
     com/2014/12/02/the-top-10-secrets-of-the-brooklyn-
     bridge/.

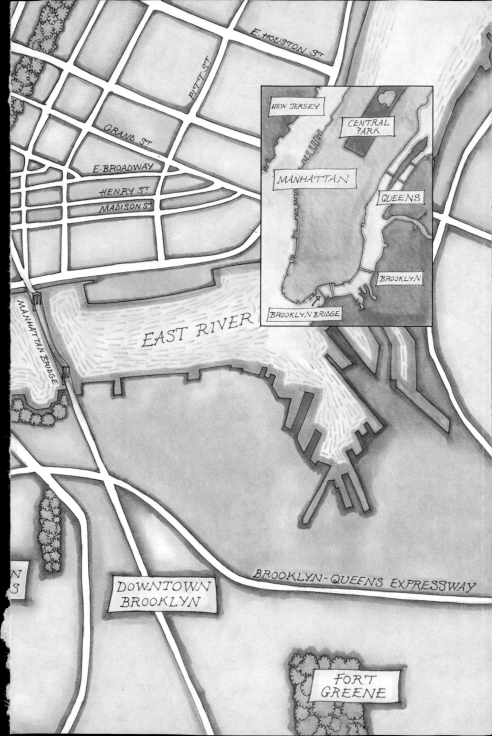

View of Manhattan skyline and the Brooklyn Bridge

View of the Brooklyn Bridge, facing Manhattan

One of the two towers of the Brooklyn Bridge

LITTLE ITALY

CANAL ST

CHURCH ST

BROADWAY

CHINATOWN

ONE WORLD TRADE
CENTER

NEW YORK
CITY HALL

TRINITY PL

RECTOR ST

WALL ST

FDR DRIVE

BROOKLYN
BRIDGE

EAST RIVER

BROOKLYN
HEIGHTS

GOVERNORS
ISLAND